What's On Your Plate?

Snacks

Ted and Lola Schaefer

Raintree

www.raintreepublishers.co.uk

Visit our website to find out more information about **Raintree** books.

To order:
☎ Phone 44 (0) 1865 888113
▤ Send a fax to 44 (0) 1865 314091
▢ Visit the Raintree bookshop at **www.raintreepublishers.co.uk**
   to browse our catalogue and order online.

First published in Great Britain by Raintree, Halley Court, Jordan Hill, Oxford, OX2 8EJ, part of Harcourt Education.
Raintree is a registered trademark of Harcourt Education Ltd.

© Harcourt Education Ltd 2006
First published in paperback in 2007
The moral right of the proprietor has been asserted.

Editorial: Patrick Catel, Rosie Gordon, and Melanie Waldron
Design: Philippa Jenkins, Lucy Owen, and John Walker
Picture Research: Melissa Allison
Production: Chloe Bloom

Originated by Chroma Graphics (Overseas) Pte Ltd.
Printed and bound in China by South China Printing Company

Hardback:
13-digit ISBN: 978 1 4062 0261 8
10-digit ISBN: 1 406 20261 4
10 09 08 07 06
10 9 8 7 6 5 4 3 2 1

Paperback:
13-digit ISBN: 978 1 4062 0266 3
10-digit ISBN: 1 406 20266 5
10 09 08 07
10 9 8 7 6 5 4 3 2 1

British Library Cataloguing-in-Publication Data
Schaefer, Lola M., 1950-
Snacks - (What's on your plate?)
1. Snack foods - Juvenile literature 2. Natural foods - Juvenile literature 3. Nutrition - Juvenile literature
I. Title II. Schaefer, Ted, 1948-

A full catalogue record for this book is available from the British Library.

Acknowledgements
The publishers would like to thank the following for permission to reproduce photographs:
p. 21, Corbis; p. 24, Corbis/Tim Pannell; p. 25, Getty Images/Brand X; p. 7, Getty images/Rubberball Productions; p. 22, Harcourt Education Ltd/Chris Honeywell; pp. 4, 5, 9, 10, 12, 13, 14, 16, 20, 23, 26, 27, 28, 29, 21, Harcourt Education Ltd/MM Studios; pp. 12, 15, 17, 18, Harcourt Education Ltd/Tudor Photography; p. 11, Holt Studios; p. 21, NHPA/Daniel Heuclin; p. 6, PhotoEdit/Nancy Sheehan; p. 21, Photolibrary.com/Botanica; pp. 9, 19, Photolibrary.com/Foodpix.

Cover photograph of oranges reproduced with permission of Alamy/Foodfolio.

The publishers would like to thank Dr Sarah Schenker for her assistance in the preparation of this book.

Disclaimer
All the Internet addresses (URLs) given in this book were valid at the time of going to press. However, due to the dynamic nature of the Internet, some addresses may have changed, or sites may have ceased to exist since publication. While the author and publishers regret any inconvenience this may cause readers, no responsibility for an such changes can be accepted by either the author or the publishers.

The paper used to print this book comes from sustainable resources.

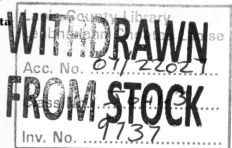
Dedicated to the memory of Lucy Owen

Contents

Any words appearing in bold, **like this,**
are explained in the Glossary.

What is a snack?

A snack is a small amount of food that you eat between meals, when you feel hungry. A snack gives you **energy**. You might want to eat one in the middle of the morning, or when you get home from school. Snacks are quick and easy to make. Usually, you can take snacks with you and eat them with your hands. Snacks can be part of a healthy **diet**.

Which of these snack foods do you like best?

In Peru, children often snack on a bowl of brazil nuts. These grow in the Amazon jungle.

Many people in Puerto Rico love mango salsa and tortilla chips. A mango is a fruit – they mix it with peppers, onions, and lime juice.

Japanese people often snack on rice crackers. They are made with healthy rice and soy sauce.

Cheese and fruit is a healthy afternoon snack, popular in France.

Why do you eat snacks?

Once a meal has been **digested** and used by the body, you can start to feel hungry again. Eating a good snack gives your body some new **energy**.

Snack foods can have different amounts of energy, which is measured in **kilojoules** or calories. The list below shows some snack foods and the amount of kilojoules (kJ) they supply.

The energy from most meals only lasts around four hours. A healthy snack will give you new energy until your next meal.

food	kilojoules	(calories)
25 g nuts and raisins	451	(108)
30 g Cheddar and four crackers	1216	(290)
apple and 1 tbsp peanut butter	701	(168)
cereal bar and glass of low fat milk	1039	(246)

g = grams/tbsp = tablespoons

Eating food gives you energy for everything you do. Awake or asleep, moving or sitting still, you use energy all the time.

The more active you are, the more energy you use up.

making a bed
(3 minutes)   13 kJ (3 cal)

dancing
(15 minutes)   142 kJ (38 cal)

hide and seek
(30 minutes)   238 kJ (57 cal)

skipping
(20 minutes)   263 kJ (63 cal)

playing tag
(30 minutes)   284 kJ (68 cal)

playing football
(20 minutes)   376 kJ (95 cal)

Energy used per activity

Quiz
How many kilojoules would your body use if you skipped for an hour?

(Answer at the bottom of the page.)

Answer: You would use 789 kJ (189 cal) in one hour while skipping.

What are the healthiest snack foods?

A healthy **diet** includes a variety of foods every day, even for snacks. You need to eat different foods because they all give you different nutrients.

The food groups needed for a healthy diet are shown in this chart.

This chart divides food into different groups. The chart can help you choose snacks from food groups you have not had in your meals, so that your diet is healthy.

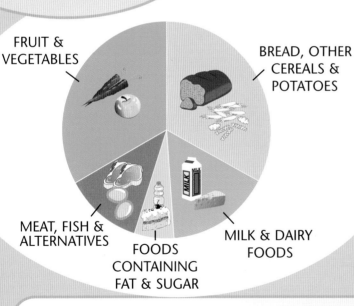

FRUIT & VEGETABLES

BREAD, OTHER CEREALS & POTATOES

MEAT, FISH & ALTERNATIVES

FOODS CONTAINING FAT & SUGAR

MILK & DAIRY FOODS

The chart above shows that some food groups should make up a smaller amount of your daily diet. If you use this chart, you can make sure that you get the food balance right.

The four main groups also contain healthy foods that can be used as snacks. The chart below shows some snack foods divided into these food groups. These foods contain all the fat and sugar you need. Select one or two snacks from different groups each day.

Bread, other cereals, and potatoes	Fruits...	...and vegetables	Milk and dairy foods	Meat, fish, and alternatives
whole grain crackers	fresh fruit	carrot and pepper sticks	yoghurt	sesame bar
breadsticks	dried fruit (raisins, cherries)	cherry tomatoes	cheddar cheese	mixed nuts
cereal bar			cream cheese	spicy sausage
popcorn	frozen fruit (blueberries, strawberries)	fresh broccoli or cauliflower	fromage frais	peanut butter
	fruit smoothie			

9

Snack foods and nutrition

Food gives you **nutrient**s. Your body needs these for good health. Important nutrients include **proteins, carbohydrates, vitamins, minerals,** and **fat.**

Carbohydrates supply your body with **energy** and fibre. Your body needs proteins to make new **cells,** so that you can grow and heal. Fats provide energy and help your body take in vitamins.

raisins

celery   peanut butter

This quick and easy snack called "ants on a log" provides carbohydrates, fibre, protein, and fat.

Which snack food has the most?

Carbohydrates	Proteins	Fats
breadsticks	walnuts	sour cream dip
cereal bar	baked beans	peanut butter
potato salad	hard-boiled egg	Cheddar cheese

Your body needs vitamins to be healthy and work properly. Vitamins make your **immune system** strong, which helps protect you from illness.

Minerals are also important for good health. Some minerals help you build strong bones and teeth.

Fibre is the nutrient that moves food through your body so that you can use the nutrients. It also helps keep your **gut** healthy.

Dates are dried, sweet-tasting fruits, that have high amounts of fibre and minerals. Dates grow in large clusters on date palm trees.

Bread, other cereals, and potatoes for snacks

Bread, other cereals, and potatoes all provide **carbohydrate**, **fibre**, and some **vitamins** and **minerals**.

Carbohydrates are turned into energy by your body. Fibre is important to keep your **gut** healthy.

These foods are an important part of your daily **diet**.

Popcorn is a cereal grain. Most children in the United States eat nearly 57 litres each in a year. That's a lot of crunch and munch!

What makes it POP?

When popcorn is heated, a little water in each grain turns to steam. The steam pushes from the inside of the grain until it explodes. POP!

Snack foods can be made with many different cereal grains. Wheat, oats, rice, and other grains are used to make crackers, bread, and cereal bars. The healthiest are made with whole grains.

Foods with whole grains keep all of their natural nutrients. **Refined** grains have some nutrients, like fibre, removed.

Six small wholegrain crackers make a healthy snack that will give your body carbohydrates to make energy.

Healthy fruit and vegetables for snacks

5-A-DAY
Eat at least 5 portions of fruit and vegetables each day.

Fruit and vegetables provide many of the **nutrients** you need for a healthy **diet**. They supply **vitamins**, **minerals**, **carbohydrates**, and **fibre**. Everyone should try to eat at least five portions each day.

Avocado to guacamole

Always ask an adult to help you in the kitchen.
tbsp = tablespoons

Guacamole is a tasty dip or spread.

To make, mix in a bowl:
- the flesh of 3 ripe avocadoes, mashed
- 1 small onion, chopped finely
- 3 garlic cloves, crushed
- 1 finely chopped tomato
- 3 tbsp lemon juice
- small amount of jalopeno peppers

Mix, chill, and serve with raw vegetables, breadsticks, or tortilla chips.

guacamole

Avocadoes are rich in healthy fats and vitamin E. Many people like guacamole, made from mashed avocadoes.

14

Fruit and vegetables can make tasty and nutritious snacks. Many vegetables taste great when eaten raw. Cooked vegetables are part of most meals. But cooking destroys some of the vitamins in vegetables, such as vitamin C and folate, so it is good to eat some raw vegetables for snacks.

You could also try drinking raw vegetable juice, such as carrot or tomato.

Ask an adult to help you slice your favourite vegetables. Store them in containers in the fridge. Whenever you are hungry for a healthy snack, they are ready!

More fruit and vegetables!

Fruit makes wonderful snacks that are easy to eat and packed with **nutrients**. Fruit can be eaten fresh or dried.

Grapes - water = raisins

Ripe grapes are dried in the sun on paper trays. In 21 days, when the water in the grapes has dried up, the grapes become raisins.

Dried fruit is high in **carbohydrates** and **fibre** and tastes sweet.

Snacks around the world

Children in Belize like to snack on plantain chips. Plantains are similar to bananas in size and shape. They are sliced thinly and fried in coconut oil for a crispy snack.

Apples are a favourite food for snacking. You can eat apples whole, drink apple juice, or make delicious apple sauce.

Apple sauce is a good snack. It provides carbohydrates, fibre, vitamins A and C, and the mineral potassium.

Homemade apple sauce

Always ask an adult to help you in the kitchen.

g = grams tbsp = tablespoons
ml = millilitres

Directions:
1. Peel and quarter 4 large apples.
2. Place the apples in a large saucepan.
3. Add 100 ml of water.
4. Add 25 g sugar or 1 tbsp honey.
5. Cook over a medium heat until apples fall apart.
6. Mash the apples and stir.
7. Eat warm or cooled. Sprinkle with cinnamon, if you like.

Healthy milk and dairy foods for snacks

Foods in the "milk and dairy foods" group include milk and cheese. These foods are rich in **protein**, **vitamins** and **minerals**, and can contain **fat**.

Your body needs protein to grow and heal. Calcium and phosphorus are two minerals supplied by milk and dairy foods. These minerals and vitamin D help to keep your bones and teeth strong and healthy.

Cottage cheese mixed with fruit on crackers makes a tasty snack. It gives you nutrients from three food groups.

Snacks around the world

Children in Turkey eat dates stuffed with cream cheese and honey, topped with pistachio nuts. This snack gives them fruit, nuts, and a "milk and dairy" food.

Other foods in the "milk and dairy" group are fromage frais and yoghurt. They can all be used for healthy snacks.

Low fat yoghurt and fruit is one of the healthiest after-school snacks.

Herb soft cheese

Cream together these ingredients to make a great topping for crackers or bread.

4 tbsp of low fat cream cheese

1 tbsp of fresh herbs (chopped by an adult – herbs could be chives, or basil)

tbsp = tablespoons

People who don't eat dairy foods can use food and milk made from soya beans. This is another good way to get calcium and protein.

19

Meat, fish, and alternatives for snacks

Foods in the "meat, fish, and alternatives" group include meats, beans, fish, eggs, nuts, and seeds. They are grouped together because they are all high in **protein**. Your body uses protein to build new **cells**.

All these foods give you **vitamins**, **minerals**, and some contain **fat**. Beans, nuts, and seeds also contain good amounts of **fibre**. Look at the chart on page 8 to see that you only need small amounts of these foods.

Tuna salad and breadsticks can make a quick, tasty snack.

Nuts and seeds are great snack foods. They provide good **nutrition** for your body and are always ready to eat. People around the world enjoy many kinds of nuts and seeds.

Nuts and seeds

These are some of the nuts and seeds that people eat.

Most nuts grow on trees, like the almond and the cashew. Peanuts grow underground on plants.

peanut

cashew

almond

Shopping for healthy snacks

Fruits are great choices for healthy snacks. They taste good and give you many vitamins.

Think about your balanced **diet** when you are buying snack foods. Foods with a lot of sugar and **fat** are high in energy, but do not contain many vitamins and minerals. Sweet snacks can also be harmful to your teeth. You should not have snacks high in sugar and fat very often.

Always look after your teeth by brushing them for two minutes twice a day.

You can buy healthy snack foods from supermarkets and health food shops. Many are also available at farmers' markets.

Some foods, like muesli bars and bananas, are ready to be snacks when you buy them. Others, like nuts or dried fruit, may come in larger packages. You can divide these into smaller containers when you get home.

Large packs of food can be divided into smaller containers for easy snacks.

Prepare safe snacks

Cleaning off **germs** is the first step in preparing safe snacks. Germs are too small to see, but they can cause food to spoil and make you sick.

Always wash your hands before preparing or eating food. Make sure your work area and **cooking utensils** are clean. Wash your hands and utensils again if they touch raw meat or eggshells.

Scrubbing with hot, soapy water kills harmful germs.

Food used to make snacks should be fresh and safe. Many food packages have labels that tell when the food is too old. Don't use any food that smells bad or does not look right.

Some types of food must be kept cold to stop germs growing on them. Snacks made with these foods should be refrigerated until used.

The "use by" date on food tells you how long the food will last. After this date, the food may not be good.

Snacks to go

Some days you might need a snack in a hurry. Maybe you suddenly feel hungry or you are rushing to go somewhere. If you have prepared ahead of time, you can grab a healthy snack and go.

Ask an adult to help you cut up foods, like carrots, apples, and cheese, into bite-size pieces. Keep your snacks fresh in small bags or plastic containers.

Pick your favourite healthy foods to prepare for snacks.

Label snacks that you store with the date so you know when you bought them. Keep foods that might spoil, like fruit, vegetables, or cheese, in the fridge.

Nuts and cereal foods can safely be stored in sealed containers in the cupboard. Labelling each food makes it easier for you to find your favourite snack.

crackers

bread sticks

dried fruit

Safe on the shelf

Here are some snack foods that can be stored safely in sealed containers in the cupboard.

cereal
sesame bars
breadsticks
all kinds of nuts
nut and dried fruit mix
raisins
dried cranberries or cherries
banana chips
popcorn
muesli bars
whole grain crackers

Snack planner: tortilla roll-ups

Prepare healthy snacks before your friends arrive. Colourful roll-ups are easy to make.

Always ask an adult to help you in the kitchen.

Cooking utensils:
- table knife
- cutting board
- sharp knife

Ingredients:
- 4 tortillas
- 225 g cream cheese, softened
- 4 spring onions, diced
- 1 yellow pepper
- 4 tbsp sliced olives
- 2 handfuls of fresh spinach leaves

g = grams   tbsp = tablespoons

Tortilla roll-ups are fun to make . . . and eat! Look carefully at these slices of roll-up and see if you can find foods from the main food groups.

Directions:

1. Ask an adult to dice the onions and pepper.
2. You can wash and pat dry the spinach leaves.
3. Lay the tortillas on greaseproof paper.
4. Spread each tortilla with the soft cream cheese.
5. Sprinkle each tortilla with ¼ of the diced pepper and onion.
6. Sprinkle on 1 tbsp of the sliced olives.
7. Hand tear the spinach and place it across each tortilla.
8. Roll each tortilla tightly.
9. Cover and chill for at least two hours.
10. When ready to serve, ask an adult to cut each roll into 2 cm slices.
11. Place them on a plate and snack away.

You can make your own tortilla roll-up recipes. After spreading the cream cheese, you can add 1-2 different vegetables, some diced, cooked meat, chopped nuts or herbs. Experiment and see which roll-up filling is your favourite.

Find out for yourself

Selecting foods for a healthy diet is important, but it doesn't have to be difficult. Learn the basic food groups and how much you need from each one. Make good choices and enjoy good health.

Books to read

Look after yourself: Get Some Exercise!, Angela Royston (Heinemann Library, 2004)

Look after yourself: Eat Healthy Food!, Angela Royston (Heinemann Library, 2004)

Go Facts: Healthy Eating, Paul McEvoy (A & C Black, 2005)

Healthy Body Cookbook: Fun Activities and Delicious Recipes for Kids, Joan D'Amico and Karen Eich Drummond (John Wiley & Sons, 1998)

Using the Internet

Explore the Internet to find out more about healthy snack foods. Websites can change so if some of the links below no longer work, don't worry. Use a search engine, such as **www.yahooligans.com** or **www.internet4kids.com** and type in key words such as "snack foods," "healthy diet" or "snack nutrition."

Websites

www.nutrition.org.uk Click on "Education", then "Cook club" for some great recipe ideas.

www.eatwell.gov.uk There is lots of information about diet and health here, as well as quizzes and games.

www.5aday.nhs.uk Find out easy ways to get your 5-a-day, and some delicious smoothie recipes.

Glossary

carbohydrate a type of nutrient in food that gives you energy

cell the body's smallest building block of living tissue

cooking utensils the knives, spoons, spatulas, and small tools that you use to prepare food

diet what you usually eat and drink

digestion the way food is broken down and used by your body

energy the power needed for your body to work and stay alive

fat a type of nutrient from food that gives you energy

fibre material in foods that is not digested but helps carry the food through the gut

germ a small living organism that can cause disease

gut the parts of your body your food travels through

immune system the part of your body that protects you from disease and infection

kilojoule a measurement of food energy

lean meat with very little fat

mineral a type of nutrient needed to make the body work correctly

nutrient substances in food (such as a vitamin, mineral, or protein) that people need to be healthy

nutrition the part of food that your body can use

protein a type of nutrient in food that gives you energy and is used for growth and repair

vitamin a type of nutrient in food that the body needs to stay healthy and to work correctly

whole grains grains, such as oats, wheat, corn, or rice, that have all or most of their natural fibre and nutrients

Index